Digital Privacy & Cyber Laws Worldwide

Understand Your Rights, Data Regulations (like GDPR), and How to Stay Compliant Across Borders

By Joe Correa

Published by Live Stronger Faster

This book is for educational and informational purposes only. The author and publisher are not engaged in rendering legal, financial, or other professional advice. Readers should consult a qualified professional before making any financial decisions.

First Edition

Table of Contents

Introduction

In an age where information flows across the globe at the speed of light, the concept of privacy has evolved from something we could take for granted to something we must actively protect. Just two decades ago, most personal information was locked away in filing cabinets, accessible only to those physically present. Today, your financial records, browsing history, medical files, purchase habits, and even private conversations can be accessed, stored, and analyzed in milliseconds — often by organizations you've never heard of. With this shift, the legal frameworks governing our digital privacy have had to evolve rapidly, attempting to catch up with the breakneck pace of technological innovation. This is where the subject of digital privacy and cyber laws becomes critically important.

The reality is that every click, tap, and swipe leaves a digital footprint. Sometimes, this footprint is intentionally created — like when you post a photo, buy something online, or sign up for a newsletter. Other times, it's entirely invisible to you, collected silently in the background through tracking pixels, cookies, and device fingerprinting. This data is immensely valuable, not just to advertisers and tech companies, but also to governments, hackers, and cybercriminals. The more valuable it becomes, the more critical it is to regulate who can collect it, store it, and use it — and to hold organizations accountable when they fail to protect it.

Digital privacy laws are the world's attempt to put guardrails around this invisible economy of personal data. These laws vary dramatically by country and jurisdiction. In the European Union, the **General Data Protection Regulation (GDPR)** has set one of the highest global standards for user privacy, granting individuals the right to access, correct, and delete their personal data, as well as the ability to object to certain uses of that data. In California, the **California Consumer Privacy Act (CCPA)** offers similar protections, with strong requirements for disclosure and the right to opt out of the sale of personal information. Brazil's **LGPD**, Canada's **PIPEDA**, and countless other frameworks around the world create a patchwork of regulations that businesses and individuals must navigate if they want to operate online without legal risk.

However, these laws don't just impact big corporations. They affect small businesses, freelancers, content creators, app developers, and even nonprofit organizations. If you collect an email address from a customer in Europe, GDPR applies to you, even if you're based in the United States or Asia. If you sell products to California residents, you are bound by the CCPA's disclosure requirements. This means that understanding cyber laws isn't just for legal professionals —

it's essential knowledge for anyone with an online presence, whether that's a website, a YouTube channel, an online store, or a global tech company.

The complexity arises when businesses operate across borders. Data is often stored in cloud servers that could be located anywhere in the world. An e-commerce site in Singapore might use a payment processor in the U.S., a cloud host in Germany, and an email marketing provider in Australia — each location introducing its own set of privacy laws. This cross-border reality creates compliance challenges but also opportunities for businesses to choose privacy-friendly providers and build trust with their customers by going above and beyond the legal minimums. The organizations that prioritize privacy often find themselves with a competitive advantage, as consumers increasingly choose to work with companies that respect and protect their personal information.

In this book, we will break down the complex web of digital privacy laws into clear, practical guidance. You'll learn the foundational principles behind major regulations like GDPR, CCPA, LGPD, and PIPEDA. We'll explore how to draft privacy policies that actually protect you legally instead of serving as meaningless boilerplate. You'll discover how to create transparent consent forms, handle data breach notifications, and securely transfer data across international borders. We'll also look at real-world cases where companies have faced massive fines for non-compliance, highlighting the lessons you can learn to avoid making the same mistakes.

Perhaps most importantly, we will shift your perspective from seeing compliance as a burden to seeing it as a trust-building tool. The most successful online businesses of the future will be those that customers trust with their data. This trust isn't built overnight — it comes from consistent, transparent, and responsible handling of personal information. Laws will continue to evolve, but if you operate with a privacy-first mindset, you will not only stay ahead of legal changes, you'll also position yourself as a leader in ethical digital business practices. By the time you finish this book, you'll have the knowledge and strategies to navigate the complex world of cyber laws with confidence, no matter where you or your customers are located.

Chapter 1: The Foundations of Digital Privacy Laws

Digital privacy laws exist to create a legal framework for how personal data can be collected, stored, processed, and shared. They are designed to protect individuals from the misuse of their information while giving them control over how that information is used. In today's interconnected world, data flows do not respect borders — which is why governments have developed comprehensive privacy regulations that apply not only within their territories but also to foreign businesses that process their citizens' data. These laws aim to prevent unauthorized use, improve transparency, and ensure that individuals have a say in how their data is handled.

The most important concept to understand is **personal data**. This term generally refers to any information that can directly or indirectly identify an individual. This includes obvious identifiers like names, addresses, phone numbers, and email addresses, as well as less obvious ones such as IP addresses, device IDs, geolocation data, and behavioral patterns. Some laws also define **sensitive personal data** — like medical records, biometric identifiers, racial or ethnic origin, political opinions, or religious beliefs — which require stronger protection and stricter handling procedures.

A second key concept is **data processing**. Processing includes any action performed on personal data, whether automated or manual. This could be collecting an email address through a web form, storing customer records in a CRM, analyzing website visitor behavior, or sharing user data with a third-party marketing service. Many organizations mistakenly believe that data protection laws only apply when they actively sell or trade data, but in reality, simply storing or using personal information in any way qualifies as processing under most legal definitions.

Globally, some laws are **comprehensive** while others are **sector-specific**. For example, the European Union's GDPR is a comprehensive law applying to almost all types of data processing, regardless of industry. In contrast, the United States has no single nationwide privacy law, but instead uses a sectoral approach: HIPAA protects health information, GLBA covers financial institutions, and COPPA governs data collected from children under 13. States like California, Colorado, and Virginia have enacted their own consumer privacy laws that apply across industries. For any business operating online, it's important to understand both the broad and niche regulations that might apply.

One of the central pillars of most privacy laws is **user consent**. Under GDPR, for example, consent must be freely given, specific, informed, and unambiguous. This means pre-checked boxes or vague language are not acceptable. Similarly, under CCPA, users have the right to opt out of the sale of their personal information. Understanding how to obtain and document consent is essential, because improperly obtained consent can invalidate your entire compliance strategy and lead to penalties.

Another critical element is **data subject rights**. These are the rights granted to individuals regarding their personal information. They often include the right to access their data, correct inaccuracies, request deletion ("right to be forgotten"), restrict processing, and receive their data in a portable format. Businesses must establish clear processes to respond to these requests within legally mandated timeframes. Failure to comply can result in substantial fines and reputational damage.

Equally important are the **accountability and transparency requirements**. Most laws require organizations to publish a clear and accessible privacy policy that explains what data they collect, why they collect it, how it's stored, and with whom it's shared. They may also require organizations to appoint a Data Protection Officer (DPO) or designate someone responsible for compliance. Beyond documentation, companies must actively demonstrate compliance through audits, employee training, and technical safeguards such as encryption and access controls.

Cross-border data transfers represent one of the most challenging aspects of privacy compliance. When data moves from one country to another, it may lose the legal protections it had in its original location unless specific safeguards are in place. The EU, for instance, allows data transfers only to countries with "adequate" privacy protections or when organizations use mechanisms like Standard Contractual Clauses (SCCs). Businesses that operate internationally must plan for these transfers carefully to avoid violations.

Finally, enforcement of privacy laws is growing stronger worldwide. Regulators are increasing audits, investigations, and penalties. The GDPR allows for fines of up to €20 million or 4% of annual global turnover, whichever is higher. The CCPA also provides for civil penalties and, in some cases, private lawsuits by consumers. This makes compliance not just a legal necessity but a strategic imperative for any organization that values its reputation and customer trust.

Understanding these foundational concepts — personal data, processing, consent, rights, accountability, and cross-border transfers — will prepare you for the more advanced compliance strategies covered in later chapters. By establishing a privacy-first mindset now, you will be better equipped to navigate the rapidly changing legal landscape and protect both your organization and the individuals whose data you handle.

Lets go over Sofia's story

Sofia ran a small but growing online design business from her apartment in Lisbon. Her customers came from all over the world, and her website proudly displayed testimonials from satisfied clients in Europe, North America, and Asia. She thought of herself as a creative entrepreneur, not a legal expert, so when she built her website, she focused on aesthetics, not privacy policies. She had a simple contact form, an online portfolio, and a store where customers could purchase design templates.

One afternoon, she received an unexpected email. It was from a customer in Germany requesting a copy of all personal information Sofia's business had stored about them. The email cited "GDPR Article 15" — something Sofia had never heard of. Confused, she searched online and discovered that the General Data Protection Regulation applied to her, even though she was a one-woman business with no physical office outside Portugal. Just by having clients in the EU, she was bound by the law's strict requirements.

As she dug deeper, Sofia realized that her website's analytics tool was collecting IP addresses, her payment processor stored customer billing information, and her email marketing software tracked who opened her newsletters. All of this counted as "personal data" under GDPR, and she was legally responsible for managing it properly. It dawned on her that privacy laws weren't just for big tech companies like Google and Facebook — they applied to her as much as to them.

The more she read, the more she understood the concept of "data processing." Every time she collected an email address, saved an invoice, or reviewed analytics, she was processing personal data. Her payment processor was a third-party data processor, and her email marketing service was another. These vendors were part of her compliance responsibility, which meant she had to ensure they followed the law, too.

Her next discovery was the principle of consent. She realized that her contact form and newsletter sign-up box lacked proper consent language. Under GDPR, consent had to be freely given, specific, informed, and unambiguous. That meant no pre-checked boxes and no vague promises. She had to clearly explain what she would do with the data and why she was collecting it.

As she worked through her compliance checklist, Sofia began

to see the bigger picture. Privacy laws weren't just bureaucratic obstacles; they were tools to build trust. She updated her privacy policy to make it understandable to her customers, implemented a process to respond to data access and deletion requests, and started encrypting stored data. She even contacted her third-party service providers to confirm their compliance measures.

A few weeks later, another client — this time from California — reached out to ask about opting out of data sales under the CCPA. Sofia didn't sell data, but she learned that even saying "we don't sell personal information" was a compliance requirement. She realized that understanding global privacy laws gave her a competitive edge. Clients appreciated her transparency, and several even commented that they felt safer doing business with her.

By the time she finished her compliance overhaul, Sofia had transformed her small business into one that met the privacy standards of some of the strictest laws in the world. The experience taught her that digital privacy isn't just a legal checkbox — it's an essential part of running a modern business. She now viewed data as a valuable asset entrusted to her by her customers, and she was determined to protect it with the same care she put into her designs.

Chapter 2: Understanding the GDPR: Europe's Gold Standard for Data Protection

The **General Data Protection Regulation (GDPR)** is widely regarded as the most comprehensive and influential privacy law in the world. Enforced since May 25, 2018, it governs how personal data of individuals in the European Union (EU) and the European Economic Area (EEA) can be collected, stored, processed, and transferred. Its reach extends far beyond Europe's borders because it applies to any organization — anywhere in the world — that offers goods or services to people in the EU or monitors their behavior. This extraterritorial scope has made GDPR a model for other laws around the globe.

At its core, GDPR is built around **seven key principles**: lawfulness, fairness, and transparency; purpose limitation; data minimization; accuracy; storage limitation; integrity and confidentiality; and accountability. These principles act as a foundation for compliance and influence every aspect of how organizations handle data. For example, "purpose limitation" means you can only collect data for a specific, legitimate purpose, and you cannot use it later for an unrelated reason without additional consent. "Data minimization" requires collecting only the data you truly need, reducing the risk of misuse or breaches.

Lawful bases for processing data are another critical element of GDPR. An organization must have a valid legal reason for collecting and processing personal information. GDPR recognizes six lawful bases: consent, contract, legal obligation, vital interests, public task, and legitimate interests. For most businesses, consent or legitimate interests are the most relevant, but each must be evaluated carefully to avoid misuse. Importantly, consent must be informed, specific, and freely given — pre-checked boxes, vague terms, or hidden opt-ins are not allowed.

GDPR also provides individuals — called **data subjects** — with powerful rights. These include the right to access their personal data, correct inaccuracies, request deletion ("right to be forgotten"), restrict processing, receive their data in a portable format, and object to certain processing activities. Businesses must respond to these requests promptly, usually within one month, and must be able to verify the identity of the requester.

Transparency is a cornerstone of GDPR. Organizations must clearly inform individuals about what data is collected, why it's collected, how it will be used, how long it will be stored, and with whom it may be shared. This is typically achieved through a detailed privacy policy, but GDPR requires that it be written in clear, understandable language, avoiding overly complex legal jargon.

Security under GDPR is addressed through the concept of "appropriate technical and organizational measures." This means businesses must implement safeguards like encryption, pseudonymization, secure storage, limited access controls, and regular security audits. The level of protection should be proportional to the sensitivity of the data being processed and the potential risk to individuals if that data is compromised.

One of GDPR's most discussed aspects is its **data breach notification requirement**. Organizations must report certain types of data breaches to their supervisory authority within 72 hours of becoming aware of the incident. If the breach poses a high risk to individuals' rights and freedoms, those individuals must also be informed without undue delay. This requirement has pushed organizations to adopt better incident response plans and monitoring tools.

Enforcement of GDPR is serious. Supervisory authorities in each EU member state can investigate complaints, conduct audits, and impose fines. Penalties can be as high as €20 million or 4% of the organization's annual global turnover, whichever is greater. These penalties apply even to small businesses and nonprofits if they fail to comply. Publicized fines have targeted both multinational corporations and small companies, demonstrating that no organization is too small to escape scrutiny.

To comply with GDPR, organizations should follow a structured approach: map all personal data processing activities, determine the lawful basis for each, update privacy policies, ensure proper consent mechanisms, secure data with technical measures, train employees, and create processes for handling data subject requests. Compliance is an ongoing process — as your business changes, your data handling practices must be reviewed and updated.

By understanding GDPR's scope, principles, lawful bases, rights, and enforcement, you can not only avoid costly penalties but also build trust with your audience. Many businesses have found that adopting GDPR standards — even if they are not legally required to — sets them apart as trustworthy and privacy-conscious, giving them a competitive advantage in the global market.

Lucas and his software company

Lukas owned a boutique software company in Canada that specialized in productivity tools for small businesses. His main customers were in North America, but over the years, his products had begun attracting attention from Europe. He never gave much thought to privacy laws outside Canada, assuming they didn't apply to him. That changed the day he received an email from a Dutch customer asking to have their account deleted and all personal data erased — citing "rights under the GDPR."

Curious, Lukas began researching and quickly realized that GDPR applied to his business because he had European customers. It didn't matter that he had no office in the EU; the fact that he offered his services to EU residents was enough. The law's extraterritorial reach meant he was suddenly responsible for meeting one of the strictest privacy standards in the world.

At first, Lukas was overwhelmed. The GDPR text was dense, filled with unfamiliar terms like "data minimization," "lawful basis," and "data subject rights." But as he broke it down, he began to understand the logic. The law wasn't designed to punish businesses arbitrarily; it was meant to protect people from having their personal information misused or mishandled.

He started by mapping every piece of personal data his company collected. This included email addresses for logins,

IP addresses recorded by his servers, payment details stored by a third-party processor, and behavioral analytics from his app. For each type of data, he asked: "Why are we collecting this?" and "Do we have a lawful basis?" In many cases, the answer was yes — contractual necessity for logins, legitimate interest for basic analytics — but for some marketing activities, he realized he needed explicit consent.

Next, Lukas overhauled his privacy policy. The old version was a generic template full of legalese. The new one explained in plain language exactly what data was collected, how it was used, how long it was kept, and how users could request its deletion. He also updated his sign-up process to include clear consent checkboxes, with links to the privacy policy and an explanation of how to withdraw consent at any time.

Security was another challenge. Although his company already used secure servers, he decided to implement encryption for stored data and limit access to personal information only to employees who needed it for their work. He also put a plan in place for responding to data breaches, including an internal protocol for reporting incidents within hours, not days.

The changes took months to implement, but the benefits were immediate. European customers expressed appreciation for the transparency, and even North American users said they felt more confident using the product. Lukas found that the process of complying with GDPR forced his company to be more organized, more transparent, and more respectful of customer data.

A year later, when a minor security incident occurred — a misconfigured server exposing a small portion of non-sensitive data — Lukas's team responded quickly. They documented the incident, notified the relevant authority within 72 hours, and informed the affected users. The incident could have been a disaster, but instead, it became an opportunity to prove their commitment to privacy. Customers responded with praise rather than criticism, and Lukas realized that GDPR compliance had transformed from a legal requirement into a powerful trust-building tool.

Chapter 3: The CCPA and U.S. State Privacy Laws: Protecting American Consumers

The **California Consumer Privacy Act (CCPA)**, effective January 1, 2020, is the most significant privacy law in the United States and has set a precedent for other states to follow. While the U.S. lacks a single comprehensive federal privacy law like Europe's GDPR, the CCPA represents a growing shift toward stronger consumer data rights at the state level. The law applies to for-profit businesses that operate in California and meet at least one of the following criteria: annual gross revenues over $25 million; buy, sell, or share the personal information of 100,000 or more consumers or households; or derive 50% or more of their annual revenue from selling consumers' personal information.

CCPA's primary objective is to give consumers more control over their personal information. It defines personal information broadly, covering identifiers such as names, addresses, email addresses, and IP addresses, as well as biometric data, browsing history, geolocation data, and inferences drawn from this information to create a consumer profile. Unlike some privacy laws, CCPA does not require a lawful basis for processing; instead, it focuses on transparency and consumer choice.

Under CCPA, California residents have several important rights. They have the **right to know** what personal information is being collected about them, both in terms of categories and specific details. They also have the **right to delete** personal information held by a business, with certain exceptions. The **right to opt out** allows consumers to prevent businesses from selling their personal information, and companies must provide a clear and conspicuous "Do Not Sell My Personal Information" link on their websites if they engage in data sales. Additionally, consumers have the **right to non-discrimination**, meaning they cannot be denied services or charged different prices simply for exercising their privacy rights.

A unique aspect of the CCPA is its focus on **opt-out mechanisms**. Unlike GDPR, which often requires opt-in consent, CCPA presumes that data collection is permissible unless the consumer opts out. This difference makes it crucial for businesses to have clear procedures for honoring opt-out requests, including verifying the identity of the person making the request. The **California Privacy Rights Act (CPRA)**, which took effect in 2023, expanded CCPA's scope by adding new rights such as the right to correct inaccurate information and by creating the California Privacy Protection Agency (CPPA) to enforce the law.

Enforcement under CCPA is carried out by the California Attorney General and, under CPRA, the CPPA. Fines for non-compliance can be significant: up to $2,500 per violation or $7,500 for intentional violations. In addition, CCPA includes a private right of action for consumers in cases of certain data breaches, allowing them to seek statutory damages between $100 and $750 per incident. This legal risk has prompted many businesses to proactively enhance their security and privacy practices.

Although CCPA is the most well-known, it is not the only U.S. state privacy law. States like Virginia, Colorado, Connecticut, and Utah have passed their own privacy acts, each with unique definitions, rights, and compliance obligations. This patchwork approach means that businesses operating nationwide must adapt their privacy strategies to comply with multiple frameworks simultaneously. In practice, many companies choose to adopt the highest standard across all states to avoid maintaining multiple compliance systems.

For compliance, businesses should start by mapping the personal information they collect and determining whether CCPA applies to them. They must update their privacy policies to include the required disclosures, implement opt-out mechanisms where applicable, train employees on handling consumer requests, and establish systems for responding to access, deletion, and correction requests within 45 days. Implementing clear and simple consumer-facing tools for privacy requests not only ensures legal compliance but also builds trust and loyalty.

While CCPA and other state laws can seem fragmented compared to GDPR, they represent an important trend toward greater accountability in the U.S. data economy. As more states pass their own laws — and pressure for a federal privacy standard grows — businesses that take compliance seriously now will be better prepared for the future.

Now, lets go over Maya's online subscription story

In the heart of Los Angeles, Maya ran an online subscription service for organic skincare products. Her business had grown quickly, attracting thousands of customers across the U.S., including a loyal base in California. She focused on product quality and customer experience, never thinking much about privacy laws until an email arrived from the California Attorney General's office. It was a notice reminding her of her obligations under the **California Consumer Privacy Act**.

At first, Maya was confused. She wasn't selling personal information, so why did the law apply to her? As she dug into the CCPA, she realized that "selling" data under the law had a broader definition than she expected. Even sharing customer information with an advertising network for targeted marketing could count as a sale. Since she used a popular ad platform to retarget website visitors, she fell under the CCPA's scope.

Maya learned that California consumers had the right to know exactly what personal information she was collecting and how it was used. They could also request deletion of their information or opt out of its sale altogether. She needed to add a "Do Not Sell My Personal Information" link to her website, update her privacy policy, and create a process for handling customer requests. She realized she had just 45 days to respond to these requests once received, so she built a small internal team to manage them.

The process wasn't easy. Her marketing director worried that honoring opt-out requests would reduce the effectiveness of their advertising campaigns. But Maya decided that customer trust was more important than short-term ad performance. She believed that being transparent would ultimately attract more loyal customers.

Around the same time, Maya discovered that other states were passing similar laws. Virginia, Colorado, and Utah each had their own versions, and while they were similar to CCPA in many respects, they all had subtle differences. Rather than managing separate compliance processes for each state, Maya decided to apply California's high standard across the board. It was more work upfront, but it simplified operations and gave all her customers the same rights, regardless of where they lived.

Months later, Maya's approach paid off. A customer from San Francisco publicly praised her company for its transparency after easily opting out of targeted ads. That post went viral in a small but influential community of eco-conscious shoppers. Orders spiked, not because of a flashy marketing campaign, but because of trust. Her brand became known not just for clean skincare, but for clean data practices.

Maya's experience taught her that privacy laws weren't obstacles to growth — they were opportunities to differentiate her brand. In an industry where many companies were slow to adapt, she positioned herself as a leader in consumer respect and data ethics. The CCPA had started as a compliance challenge, but it ended up becoming a cornerstone of her company's competitive advantage.

Chapter 4: Brazil's LGPD and the Rise of Latin American Privacy Laws

The **Lei Geral de Proteção de Dados Pessoais** (LGPD) is Brazil's comprehensive data protection law, modeled closely after the European Union's GDPR. It came into effect in September 2020 and applies to any individual or organization — inside or outside Brazil — that processes personal data in Brazil or offers goods or services to people located in the country. The LGPD is significant not only because Brazil is the largest economy in Latin America, but also because it signals the region's growing focus on privacy and data protection.

Like GDPR, the LGPD defines **personal data** broadly to include any information related to an identified or identifiable natural person, whether directly or indirectly. It also introduces the concept of **sensitive personal data**, which covers information about racial or ethnic origin, religious beliefs, political opinions, union membership, health or sexual orientation, and biometric or genetic data. Processing sensitive data requires additional safeguards and, in most cases, explicit consent.

The LGPD is built on **ten legal bases for data processing**, which are similar to GDPR's lawful bases but tailored to Brazilian legal culture. These include consent, legal obligation, contract performance, legitimate interest, and protection of credit, among others. Consent under the LGPD must be free, informed, and unambiguous. Data subjects must be able to revoke consent easily, and revocation should be as simple as granting it.

One of the LGPD's standout features is its strong emphasis on **data subject rights**. Brazilian citizens and residents have the right to confirm the existence of processing, access their data, correct inaccuracies, request anonymization or deletion, and obtain portability of their data to another service or product provider. They also have the right to be informed about the public and private entities with which their data has been shared. Businesses must be prepared to respond to such requests promptly and transparently.

The LGPD requires organizations to appoint a **Data Protection Officer (DPO)**, responsible for overseeing compliance and serving as the primary contact for the national data protection authority – the **Autoridade Nacional de Proteção de Dados** (ANPD). This role is critical in ensuring that data protection measures are integrated into the organization's operations and culture.

Data security under LGPD is framed as the duty to adopt technical and administrative measures capable of protecting personal data from unauthorized access and accidental or unlawful destruction, loss, alteration, communication, or dissemination. While the law does not prescribe specific technologies, it emphasizes proportionality – the measures taken should match the sensitivity and volume of the data being processed.

Violations of the LGPD can result in significant penalties. The ANPD may impose fines of up to 2% of a company's revenue in Brazil, capped at 50 million Brazilian reais (approximately $10 million USD) per infraction. Sanctions can also include publicizing the infraction, blocking personal data, or ordering its deletion. These penalties have made privacy compliance a high priority for businesses in Brazil and those interacting with Brazilian consumers.

Beyond Brazil, several Latin American countries – including Argentina, Chile, Colombia, and Mexico – have passed or are in the process of updating their privacy laws to align more closely with global standards like GDPR. For businesses operating in the region, this means adopting a harmonized privacy strategy that accounts for both LGPD and local laws.

For compliance, organizations should conduct a data mapping exercise to understand what Brazilian personal data they process, determine the legal basis for processing, update privacy notices, implement consent mechanisms, and establish protocols for responding to data subject requests. Given the LGPD's similarities to GDPR, companies already compliant with GDPR will find adaptation easier, but they must still address the law's unique provisions.

By embracing LGPD's requirements, organizations not only avoid costly fines but also position themselves as trustworthy partners in a region where digital trust is still developing. In markets like Brazil, where personal relationships and reputation are critical to business success, demonstrating a commitment to privacy can create a significant competitive advantage.

Diego's e-commerce story

Diego owned a mid-sized e-commerce company in São Paulo that sold handmade furniture across Brazil and to customers abroad. His online store had been steadily growing, with orders coming in from the U.S., Europe, and Asia. For years, he had managed customer data casually — saving order details, storing email addresses for marketing, and tracking website visits to improve his site. Privacy policies were an afterthought, something he copied from another website and never updated.

Everything changed when the **Lei Geral de Proteção de Dados Pessoais** (LGPD) went into effect. Diego first heard about it from a friend who worked at a tech company. "It's Brazil's version of GDPR," the friend explained, "and it's serious. The fines are huge." At first, Diego thought it only applied to large corporations. But when he learned that any business processing personal data in Brazil fell under the law, he realized he couldn't ignore it.

Diego began researching LGPD and quickly saw the gaps in his own practices. He discovered that his business collected not just names and addresses, but also phone numbers, payment information, and detailed purchase histories. This was all considered personal data under LGPD. Even more concerning, his analytics tool collected IP addresses and browsing behavior, and he had no formal consent mechanism for any of it.

One provision caught his attention: the requirement to appoint a **Data Protection Officer (DPO)**. As a small business owner, he couldn't hire a full-time specialist, so he decided to take on the role himself. He studied the law, took online training courses, and began developing new data handling policies. He updated his website to include a clear, plain-language privacy policy and added a pop-up banner requesting consent for analytics cookies.

Customers began to notice the changes. One emailed to thank Diego for explaining how their data was being used and giving them the option to opt out of marketing emails. Another asked for a copy of all data Diego's company had stored about them — a request that once would have baffled him. Now, he was able to respond quickly, providing a secure downloadable file within a few days.

At first, some of his staff grumbled about the extra work. But over time, they began to see the benefits. Customer complaints about unwanted emails dropped, and trust in the brand increased. International buyers, especially those from Europe, expressed confidence in purchasing from his store, knowing that it followed strict privacy rules.

Six months later, a competitor in the same industry made headlines for an LGPD violation after exposing customer data in an unsecured database. The news spread quickly, and many of that competitor's customers switched to Diego's store. The compliance work that once felt like a burden had become one of his strongest selling points.

Diego realized that LGPD wasn't just about avoiding fines — it was about respecting the people who trusted him with their personal information. In Brazil's competitive e-commerce market, that respect translated into loyalty, referrals, and steady growth.

Chapter 5: Canada's PIPEDA and North American Cross-Border Data Rules

The **Personal Information Protection and Electronic Documents Act** (PIPEDA) is Canada's federal privacy law for private-sector organizations. First enacted in 2000 and later expanded, PIPEDA applies to organizations engaged in commercial activities across most provinces and territories, with some provinces (like British Columbia, Alberta, and Quebec) having their own laws deemed "substantially similar" to PIPEDA. Businesses in these provinces must comply with their respective laws, but PIPEDA still applies when personal data crosses provincial or national borders.

PIPEDA defines **personal information** broadly as any information about an identifiable individual, excluding business contact information in certain contexts. Examples include names, home addresses, Social Insurance Numbers, medical records, financial details, and opinions about an individual. Unlike the GDPR or Brazil's LGPD, PIPEDA focuses heavily on the principle of **meaningful consent** – ensuring individuals understand what information is being collected, why it's being collected, and how it will be used before agreeing to it.

The law is built on **ten fair information principles** that guide how organizations should manage personal data:

1. Accountability
2. Identifying purposes
3. Consent
4. Limiting collection
5. Limiting use, disclosure, and retention
6. Accuracy
7. Safeguards
8. Openness
9. Individual access
10. Challenging compliance

These principles require organizations to appoint someone responsible for compliance, clearly state the purposes of data collection, and limit both the scope and duration of data retention. For example, businesses cannot collect data "just in case" it might be useful later — they must have a specific, stated purpose.

PIPEDA allows for both **express** and **implied consent**, but the law requires express consent for sensitive personal information and in situations where the individual would not reasonably expect their data to be used. Implied consent might apply when a customer provides their address for delivery, implying they consent to its use for shipping purposes. However, businesses must always be transparent and avoid burying consent terms in long, inaccessible privacy policies.

An important aspect of PIPEDA is its application to **cross-border data transfers**. If an organization transfers personal data to a service provider in another country, it must ensure comparable protection through contractual agreements and due diligence. While PIPEDA does not prohibit cross-border transfers, it requires businesses to notify individuals that their data may be processed in another jurisdiction, which could be subject to different laws and access requests by foreign governments.

Security under PIPEDA is defined through **appropriate safeguards** relative to the sensitivity of the data. These safeguards may include encryption, secure storage, employee training, and restricted access. PIPEDA also includes breach notification requirements: organizations must report any breach of security safeguards that poses a "real risk of significant harm" to the Office of the Privacy Commissioner of Canada (OPC) and notify affected individuals as soon as possible.

Non-compliance with PIPEDA can lead to public investigations, reputational damage, and, in serious cases, court actions resulting in damages. While fines under PIPEDA have historically been less severe than GDPR or LGPD penalties, proposed reforms aim to increase enforcement powers and penalties, making compliance even more critical.

For businesses, compliance involves identifying what personal information is collected, obtaining meaningful consent, securing data with appropriate safeguards, being transparent about policies, and training employees on handling personal information. Businesses with cross-border operations must take extra care to meet both Canadian and foreign requirements.

By understanding and applying PIPEDA's principles, organizations can protect privacy while enabling international business. In an increasingly global digital economy, transparency and trust are as important as the products and services offered.

The story of Amira's digital marketing agency

Amira ran a boutique digital marketing agency in Toronto, serving clients across Canada, the U.S., and Europe. Her small team handled everything from website design to email campaigns, and their clients often provided them with customer lists for marketing. For years, Amira assumed that because she worked mainly with Canadian companies, privacy compliance wasn't a major concern. That assumption changed when one of her clients asked her to ensure all their campaigns complied with **PIPEDA**.

Curious, Amira began researching the law and quickly realized that her agency was already processing significant amounts of personal information: names, emails, purchase histories, and even behavioral tracking data from website analytics. Under PIPEDA, all of this counted as personal information, and it came with legal obligations.

The first step was appointing someone responsible for compliance. As the business owner, Amira took on the role, diving into PIPEDA's **ten fair information principles**. She discovered gaps in her processes — for example, her agency stored old customer lists indefinitely, even after campaigns ended. PIPEDA required that data be retained only as long as necessary for the purpose it was collected, so she introduced a strict data deletion policy.

Consent was another area that needed attention. Some of her clients' signup forms had vague language about how customer information would be used. Amira revised these forms to clearly explain data collection purposes, adding separate checkboxes for newsletter subscriptions and targeted advertising consent. She also implemented express consent for sensitive information, such as health-related survey responses for a wellness client.

When she learned about PIPEDA's rules for **cross-border data transfers**, Amira realized that her agency used a U.S.-based email marketing service. This meant she had to inform clients — and in turn their customers — that personal data might be stored outside Canada and subject to U.S. laws. She updated her privacy policies accordingly and reviewed the service provider's security practices.

Security was another priority. Amira introduced encrypted storage for sensitive files, enforced two-factor authentication for all team accounts, and held training sessions on recognizing phishing attempts. Her team initially found the changes cumbersome, but soon they appreciated the increased security, especially after hearing about a competitor's data breach that cost them a major client.

A few months later, one of Amira's clients faced a data breach involving stolen customer emails and passwords. Thanks to the new processes, Amira's team acted quickly: they reported the breach to the Office of the Privacy Commissioner of Canada, notified the affected individuals, and helped the client set up stronger security measures. The client praised her agency's professionalism, and word spread, leading to new contracts from businesses seeking privacy-conscious marketing services.

Amira realized that PIPEDA compliance wasn't just about avoiding fines — it was about building trust and credibility. In the competitive world of digital marketing, being able to assure clients that their data was handled with the utmost care became a powerful selling point. Over time, it helped her agency stand out in a crowded marketplace, proving that privacy could be both a responsibility and a business advantage.

Chapter 6: Data Transfer Rules and Cross-Border Compliance

In today's digital economy, data rarely stays in one place. Whether through cloud storage, remote teams, or third-party services, personal data often crosses borders — sometimes without the knowledge of the individuals it belongs to. This movement triggers a complex set of **data transfer rules** that are embedded in privacy laws worldwide. Understanding and complying with these rules is essential for avoiding legal risks and maintaining user trust.

Cross-border data transfer occurs when personal data is moved from one jurisdiction to another, physically or digitally. For example, a business in Canada that uses a U.S.-based payment processor is transferring data across borders. While this seems routine, the legal implications can be significant because privacy protections vary by country. Some jurisdictions consider certain countries "adequate" in terms of privacy protection, while others require additional safeguards.

Under the **European Union's GDPR**, personal data can only be transferred outside the EU/EEA to countries that the European Commission has deemed to provide "adequate" data protection. If a country is not on this list, organizations must use mechanisms such as **Standard Contractual Clauses**

(SCCs), **Binding Corporate Rules (BCRs)**, or explicit user consent for the transfer. The Schrems II ruling in 2020 invalidated the EU–U.S. Privacy Shield framework, making these safeguards even more important.

Brazil's **LGPD** also restricts cross-border transfers, requiring either adequate protection in the destination country or specific safeguards, such as contractual clauses approved by the Brazilian data protection authority. Similarly, **Canada's PIPEDA** allows cross-border transfers but mandates transparency, meaning individuals must be informed when their data will be processed in another country and that it may be subject to different legal regimes.

In the **United States**, there is no single federal law governing cross-border data transfers, but sector-specific regulations like HIPAA for health data and GLBA for financial data impose restrictions. Additionally, state privacy laws, such as the **California Consumer Privacy Act (CCPA)**, may require disclosures about cross-border transfers.

Security considerations are a major part of cross-border compliance. Even if the legal framework permits the transfer, organizations must ensure that the receiving entity has adequate technical and organizational safeguards. This may include encryption during transmission, limited access rights, and ongoing security audits.

Contracts and agreements are often the backbone of cross-border compliance. Standard Contractual Clauses are pre-approved legal tools that bind the data importer to meet specific privacy obligations. Binding Corporate Rules are internal policies for multinational companies that must be approved by regulators. In both cases, the goal is to ensure that data enjoys the same level of protection abroad as it would in the originating country.

Transparency with users is another critical requirement. Many privacy laws mandate that organizations clearly explain in their privacy notices whether personal data is stored or processed abroad, why it is necessary, and what protections are in place. Without this transparency, even legally permissible transfers can erode trust.

To remain compliant, businesses should map all data flows, identify when and where cross-border transfers occur, and document the legal basis for each transfer. They should also conduct due diligence on all vendors and partners to ensure they meet applicable privacy standards. By implementing these measures, organizations not only reduce legal risk but also position themselves as trustworthy stewards of personal information in a global marketplace.

Evelyn's story

Evelyn managed a health and wellness subscription service based in London. Her business provided personalized nutrition plans and shipped supplements to customers in more than 20 countries. When she first launched, she focused on marketing, product quality, and customer satisfaction, never thinking much about where her customers' data was stored.

One day, while preparing for a partnership with a U.S.-based fulfillment company, her legal consultant asked, "Where is all your customer data currently stored?" Evelyn admitted she wasn't sure — her payment processor, email marketing platform, and cloud file storage were all hosted by different providers, some of which were outside the UK and EU. That's when she learned about GDPR's strict rules on cross-border data transfers.

Her consultant explained that under GDPR, personal data could only be transferred to countries deemed to have "adequate" protections, or it needed special safeguards like **Standard Contractual Clauses**. The U.S. wasn't currently on the adequacy list, so every transfer to her American partners required either SCCs or explicit consent from customers. This meant she needed to renegotiate contracts with several vendors and add legal protections to ensure compliance.

The more she investigated, the more complex it became. Her nutrition analysis software was hosted on servers in Australia, her marketing automation tool stored customer emails in the U.S., and her data backup provider had servers in Singapore. Each of these involved a cross-border transfer with its own compliance requirements.

Evelyn decided to map all her data flows, from the moment a customer signed up to every system that touched their information. The results were eye-opening — she counted more than 15 separate cross-border transfers. With her legal consultant's help, she implemented SCCs where necessary, verified vendor security certifications, and added a clear section in her privacy policy explaining the transfers and protections.

At first, she feared that telling customers their data was processed in other countries might scare them away. Instead, the opposite happened. Customers appreciated the transparency and the effort Evelyn's company put into safeguarding their information. One long-time subscriber even wrote, "It's rare to see a company be this upfront about where my data goes. It makes me trust you more."

A year later, when an EU-based competitor faced fines for unlawful cross-border transfers, Evelyn's compliance work paid off. Regulators reviewing her processes found everything in order, and she was even invited to speak at an industry conference on global data privacy. What began as a daunting legal hurdle had turned into a marketing advantage – her company became known not only for health products, but also for respecting the privacy of customers worldwide.

Chapter 7: The Role of Data Protection Authorities and Enforcement

Data protection authorities (DPAs) are the regulatory bodies responsible for enforcing privacy and data protection laws in their respective jurisdictions. They act as both **watchdogs** and **guides**, ensuring that organizations comply with the rules while also educating the public about their rights. Understanding the role of DPAs is essential for any business or individual handling personal information because these agencies have the power to investigate complaints, conduct audits, issue fines, and, in some cases, even halt certain business activities.

Each jurisdiction has its own DPA or equivalent body. Under the **General Data Protection Regulation (GDPR)** in the European Union, every member state has its own supervisory authority — such as the CNIL in France, the ICO in the UK (before Brexit), and the BfDI in Germany. These authorities have wide-ranging powers to monitor compliance, investigate breaches, and impose administrative fines. In Brazil, the **Autoridade Nacional de Proteção de Dados** (ANPD) serves a similar role, while in Canada, it's the **Office of the Privacy Commissioner** (OPC). In the U.S., there is no single federal DPA, but agencies like the **Federal Trade**

single lead supervisory authority. Similarly, global forums like the Global Privacy Assembly (GPA) bring together regulators from different regions to coordinate enforcement efforts.

For compliance, organizations should know which DPA oversees their operations, understand the reporting requirements, and monitor any guidance issued. Keeping lines of communication open with regulators and staying informed about enforcement trends can help businesses avoid costly missteps. In an environment where privacy laws continue to evolve, DPAs are not just enforcers — they are partners in building a culture of data protection.

Mateo's unregulated story

Mateo owned a mid-sized software company in Madrid that developed customer relationship management (CRM) tools for small businesses. His platform stored client contact details, sales histories, and even notes about customer preferences. For years, Mateo operated without any direct interaction with regulators, assuming that as long as he kept his systems secure, he was in good standing. That assumption changed the day he received a letter from the **Agencia Española de Protección de Datos** (AEPD) — Spain's data protection authority.

The letter wasn't a fine, but it was a request for information. A former customer had filed a complaint alleging that Mateo's company had refused to delete their data after they closed their account. The AEPD wanted to know the company's policies for handling deletion requests, as well as proof that these policies had been followed.

Initially nervous, Mateo contacted a lawyer specializing in GDPR compliance. Together, they prepared a detailed response, including the company's data retention policy, deletion logs, and email correspondence with the complainant. In the process, Mateo realized that while his team had good intentions, they lacked formal procedures for handling such requests — making it harder to prove compliance.

The AEPD ultimately concluded that there had been no intentional wrongdoing, but they issued a warning and required Mateo's company to improve its processes. While this wasn't the outcome he had hoped for, it turned into a valuable lesson. He implemented a new system that automatically tracked and confirmed all deletion requests, complete with timestamps and audit logs.

Over time, Mateo began to see the DPA not just as an enforcer, but as a resource. He subscribed to the AEPD's newsletter, attended a webinar on GDPR compliance, and even reached out to them with questions about cross-border transfers. To his surprise, the agency responded quickly with practical guidance.

A year later, when a major security breach affected a competitor in the CRM industry, Mateo's company was ready. They detected an attempted intrusion, blocked it, and reported the incident to the AEPD within 72 hours, as required by law. The agency praised their swift response and noted their improved compliance systems. This public acknowledgment boosted Mateo's reputation among his clients, many of whom were small businesses that valued security and transparency.

What started as a stressful investigation had transformed into a working relationship. Mateo learned that a DPA's role was not to destroy businesses, but to ensure that organizations respected people's privacy rights. By viewing the regulator as a partner rather than an adversary, Mateo positioned his company as a trusted, compliant player in the competitive European tech market.

Chapter 8: How Businesses Stay Compliant: Policies, Training, and Audits

Staying compliant with digital privacy laws requires more than writing a privacy policy and hoping for the best. It is an ongoing process that involves creating clear **internal policies**, training employees to follow them, and conducting regular **audits** to identify and address gaps. Businesses that view compliance as a one-time checklist often fall out of alignment with the law, especially as regulations evolve. Those that treat it as part of their operational culture, however, can build trust, reduce legal risk, and maintain a strong market reputation.

The foundation of compliance is a **comprehensive privacy policy** — not just the public-facing version for customers, but also internal policies that govern how employees handle data. A good privacy policy should outline:

- What personal data the organization collects
- The legal basis for processing it
- How it is stored and secured
- Who it is shared with

- How long it is retained
- The process for responding to access, correction, and deletion requests This policy must be kept up to date and should reflect changes in the business's operations, technology, or applicable laws.

Equally important is **employee training**. Even the most sophisticated technical safeguards can be undermined by human error. Phishing emails, weak passwords, or careless handling of sensitive data can all lead to breaches. Training should cover the basics of data protection, the specific privacy laws relevant to the organization, and the procedures employees must follow when handling personal information. Role-specific training is often necessary — for example, customer service teams need to know how to respond to data requests, while IT teams must understand encryption and access controls.

Audits and assessments are the next layer of compliance. A privacy audit examines the organization's data processing activities to ensure they align with legal requirements and internal policies. This often involves:

- Mapping all personal data flows
- Reviewing consent mechanisms

- Checking vendor contracts for compliance clauses
- Testing security measures
- Ensuring data subject rights requests are handled promptly Audits can be conducted internally or by external consultants, and they should be performed regularly — at least annually — or whenever there are significant changes in operations or laws.

Documentation is critical to proving compliance. Many laws, such as GDPR, require organizations to demonstrate that they have taken appropriate measures to protect personal data. Keeping records of data processing activities, employee training sessions, breach response drills, and policy updates can make the difference between a quick resolution and a costly investigation.

Vendor management is another key area. Many organizations share data with third parties — payment processors, marketing agencies, cloud service providers — that act as "data processors." Businesses must ensure that these partners meet the same privacy standards they are held to. This means having contracts with clear data protection clauses, conducting due diligence, and periodically reviewing the vendor's compliance.

Finally, compliance is not static. Laws evolve, new regulations emerge, and technology changes rapidly. Businesses should assign someone — often a Data Protection Officer or compliance manager — to monitor developments, update policies, and ensure ongoing training. Treating privacy as a living, breathing part of the business culture ensures that it adapts alongside growth and innovation.

By building a compliance program that integrates policies, training, and audits into everyday operations, organizations can turn what might seem like a regulatory burden into a competitive advantage. Customers increasingly choose to work with businesses that can prove they take privacy seriously.

Nina's mandatory employee training

Nina owned a mid-sized travel booking agency in Singapore. Her company had grown rapidly, offering flights, hotel reservations, and travel insurance packages to customers worldwide. With growth came complexity — her business handled vast amounts of personal data, from passport numbers to credit card details. She knew there were privacy laws in place, but she assumed that because she used well-known third-party booking platforms, compliance was mostly their responsibility.

That assumption changed after she attended a tourism industry conference where a speaker detailed the heavy fines a travel agency in Europe had faced for failing to secure customer data. The breach hadn't been caused by hackers — it was the result of an employee emailing an unencrypted spreadsheet with thousands of customer records to the wrong person. Nina realized that no matter how secure her technology was, her team's habits could be a liability.

Determined to avoid a similar fate, Nina decided to overhaul her company's privacy practices. She started by creating a detailed **internal privacy policy**. It spelled out exactly what data the company collected, how it was stored, who could access it, and the steps required to securely delete it. She made sure every department, from sales to customer service, had specific instructions relevant to their roles.

Next, she rolled out **mandatory employee training**. Instead of making it a boring lecture, she worked with a cybersecurity consultant to create interactive sessions. Employees learned to recognize phishing attempts, use strong passwords, and securely share sensitive documents. Role-playing exercises simulated data requests from customers and regulators, giving the team confidence in responding appropriately.

To ensure the policies were working, Nina scheduled **quarterly audits**. Her team mapped out all the data flows, from the moment a customer booked a trip to the time their information was archived or deleted. They reviewed contracts with vendors and discovered that one small hotel partner lacked proper security measures. Nina negotiated new terms requiring encryption for any customer data they received.

The process wasn't always easy. Some employees resisted the changes, viewing them as extra work. But over time, the culture shifted. Staff began spotting and reporting potential issues before they became problems. During one audit, a team member caught a misconfigured setting in the booking system that could have exposed customer data — fixing it immediately prevented what could have been a serious breach.

Six months later, Nina's commitment to compliance paid off in an unexpected way. A corporate client looking for a travel agency specifically requested proof of strong privacy practices. Nina was able to provide training records, audit reports, and detailed policies, winning the contract over competitors who couldn't offer the same level of assurance.

Nina learned that privacy compliance wasn't just about avoiding penalties — it was about building trust and professionalism. By embedding policies, training, and audits into her business, she turned privacy from a box-ticking exercise into a selling point, ensuring that her company was both secure and competitive in the global travel market.

Chapter 9: Emerging Trends in Global Privacy Regulation

Digital privacy is no longer a niche legal topic — it is a global policy priority. Over the last decade, privacy laws have shifted from fragmented, industry-specific rules to comprehensive, rights-based frameworks that affect almost every business in the digital economy. This trend shows no sign of slowing down. Understanding the emerging patterns in global privacy regulation helps businesses prepare for changes before they happen, rather than scrambling to comply after the fact.

One of the most notable trends is the **convergence toward GDPR-style laws**. The European Union's General Data Protection Regulation has become the blueprint for privacy legislation worldwide. Countries in Latin America, Africa, Asia, and the Middle East are adopting laws with similar principles — such as requiring a lawful basis for processing, granting individuals broad data rights, and imposing strong accountability measures. This means that even if a business does not currently operate in the EU, it may still face GDPR-like obligations in other markets.

Another key development is the rise of **regional privacy frameworks**. The African Union's Convention on Cyber Security and Personal Data Protection, the ASEAN Framework on Personal Data Protection, and the Asia-Pacific Economic Cooperation (APEC) Privacy Framework are all examples of efforts to harmonize laws across multiple countries. While these frameworks are not always legally binding, they encourage consistency and make it easier for businesses to operate across borders with a single compliance strategy.

Technology-specific regulation is also on the rise. Governments are recognizing that certain technologies present unique privacy risks that require tailored rules. For example, laws governing biometric data, facial recognition systems, and artificial intelligence are becoming more common. The EU's proposed Artificial Intelligence Act will impose transparency and risk-assessment obligations on AI systems, while several U.S. states are considering or have passed laws restricting the use of facial recognition in public spaces.

Children's privacy protections are expanding globally. Inspired by the U.S. Children's Online Privacy Protection Act (COPPA) and reinforced by GDPR's special rules for minors, many jurisdictions are strengthening consent requirements and limiting data collection for users under a certain age. Businesses with products or services appealing to children must be prepared to verify age and obtain parental consent where necessary.

Another emerging trend is the **integration of privacy and cybersecurity laws**. While traditionally treated as separate areas, many governments now see them as interconnected. Data breach notification requirements are becoming standard worldwide, and some laws mandate specific security measures as part of privacy compliance. This blurring of lines means that businesses must coordinate their privacy and cybersecurity strategies.

Enforcement is also evolving. Regulators are increasingly cooperating across borders, sharing information, and launching joint investigations. The trend toward **higher penalties** is clear — fines under privacy laws are growing in size and frequency, with regulators showing less tolerance for repeat offenders. Additionally, some laws now give individuals the right to sue organizations directly for privacy violations, increasing the legal and financial risks.

Finally, there is a growing emphasis on **ethical data practices**. Consumers are becoming more aware of how their data is used and are rewarding companies that go beyond legal compliance to embrace transparency, fairness, and minimal data collection. Businesses that adopt a "privacy by design" approach — embedding privacy into every stage of product and service development — are more likely to gain long-term trust and loyalty.

For organizations, staying ahead of these trends requires continuous monitoring of global privacy developments, adopting flexible compliance frameworks, and prioritizing ethical data practices. Those that view privacy as a competitive advantage rather than just a legal obligation will be better positioned to thrive in the evolving digital landscape.

Now, lets go over Ravi's story

Ravi ran a small but ambitious mobile app development company in Mumbai. His flagship app, a fitness tracking platform, had grown rapidly, gaining users not only in India but also in Europe, North America, and Southeast Asia. Initially, his focus was purely on features and user experience, but as his user base expanded, so did the complexity of the privacy laws he had to navigate.

One day, he received a partnership proposal from a large Singapore-based health and wellness brand. The deal was potentially transformative for his company, but their legal team had a long list of privacy compliance questions. They wanted to know how his app handled biometric data, whether he had processes for deleting user information upon request, and if he complied with GDPR for European users. Ravi realized that while his app had some basic privacy settings, it wasn't designed with global regulations in mind.

He began researching and discovered that privacy laws were evolving rapidly across multiple regions. In Southeast Asia, the ASEAN Framework on Personal Data Protection was influencing national laws. In the EU, GDPR had strict requirements for processing sensitive health data. In California, the CCPA gave users the right to opt out of data sharing. In India, a proposed Personal Data Protection Bill was in the works, expected to align closely with international standards.

Ravi decided to adopt a **privacy by design** approach for his app. He worked with his development team to minimize data collection – storing only what was essential for the app's core functions. They added granular privacy controls, allowing users to opt in or out of specific data processing features. For biometric data like heart rate and step counts, they implemented encryption and required explicit consent before collecting it.

He also began monitoring **technology-specific regulations**. Since his app used AI-driven analytics to suggest personalized workouts, he paid close attention to the EU's proposed Artificial Intelligence Act. He realized that compliance with these emerging rules could become a selling point, especially as users became more cautious about how AI processed their data.

The changes paid off. When the Singapore wellness brand's legal team reviewed his updated policies and security measures, they were impressed. Not only did they sign the partnership deal, but they also promoted his app as a model for responsible data practices.

A year later, Ravi's proactive approach to emerging privacy trends attracted even more opportunities. An educational institution in Australia adopted his app for a student fitness program, citing its strong privacy features as the deciding factor. Ravi realized that by staying ahead of privacy regulations, he had turned what could have been a legal challenge into a competitive edge.

Chapter 10: The Future of Digital Privacy: Preparing for What's Next

The future of digital privacy will be shaped by rapid technological innovation, evolving consumer expectations, and increasingly coordinated global regulation. While the current landscape is already complex, the next decade promises even more dramatic changes. Organizations that anticipate these shifts and prepare in advance will be far better positioned than those that react only when new laws are enforced.

One of the most significant future drivers of privacy change is **emerging technology**. Artificial intelligence, blockchain, quantum computing, and the Internet of Things (IoT) are creating new ways to collect, store, and analyze personal data. AI can derive highly personal insights from seemingly harmless data points, IoT devices can gather continuous streams of information from everyday activities, and blockchain — while offering transparency — presents challenges for deletion rights due to its immutable nature. Quantum computing could eventually break current encryption standards, requiring entirely new security protocols.

Privacy laws will need to adapt quickly to these technologies. Expect to see **AI-specific transparency and**

accountability rules, tighter restrictions on biometric and genetic data, and sector-specific privacy laws targeting industries like healthcare, finance, and education. The EU's Artificial Intelligence Act, for example, may serve as a model for regulating high-risk AI systems, requiring risk assessments, human oversight, and clear explanations for algorithmic decisions.

Another trend shaping the future is **consumer empowerment**. As individuals become more aware of how their data is used, they will demand greater control and transparency. This will likely lead to expanded data subject rights, such as the ability to see exactly which algorithms are processing their data, request explanations for automated decisions, and easily port their data between service providers. Companies that make privacy controls simple and user-friendly will have a competitive advantage.

Global privacy regulation is also moving toward **greater harmonization**. While today's environment is fragmented, with different rules in different countries, there is growing pressure for standardized frameworks that make cross-border compliance simpler. Organizations like the OECD, the Global Privacy Assembly, and various trade agreements are pushing for more consistent rules to facilitate international business while protecting individuals' rights.

In addition, **privacy will increasingly merge with ethics and sustainability**. Consumers and investors are beginning to evaluate companies based on how responsibly they handle data, alongside environmental and social performance. "Privacy ratings" could become as common as ESG (Environmental, Social, and Governance) scores, influencing purchasing decisions and investment flows.

For businesses, preparing for the future means embedding **privacy by design** into every stage of operations, investing in adaptable compliance frameworks, and monitoring emerging laws and technologies. It also means rethinking data strategy — collecting only what is necessary, securing it with the most advanced tools available, and being transparent about how it is used.

Organizations that succeed in the next era of privacy will not only comply with regulations but will make privacy a defining part of their brand identity. In a world where trust is a scarce commodity, a reputation for protecting personal information may be one of the most valuable assets a company can have.

The story of how Leila anticipated the future of privacy

Leila ran a fast-growing fintech startup in Dubai that offered a digital wallet and personal finance management app. The app integrated with banks, payment processors, and e-commerce platforms, making it a convenient tool for customers — but also a treasure trove of personal and financial data.

As her business expanded internationally, Leila kept a close eye on privacy regulations in different regions. But she also wondered: what will privacy look like five or ten years from now? She decided to think beyond current compliance and prepare her company for what was coming next.

Her first step was to assess the **impact of emerging technologies** on her business. The app's AI-driven analytics could predict spending patterns and suggest savings strategies, but Leila realized these features might one day require explicit AI transparency reports under future laws. She began documenting how the AI worked and why certain recommendations were made, anticipating that regulators would eventually demand this information.

She also considered the **Internet of Things**. As wearables and connected devices became more popular, her app could potentially integrate with smartwatches, home assistants, or even connected cars to provide real-time budgeting tips. While exciting, this expansion would mean handling far more granular data — from geolocation to voice commands — all of which could be subject to stricter privacy rules.

Leila worked with her development team to adopt a **privacy**

by design approach for every new feature. They minimized data collection, built strong encryption into all systems, and made privacy settings easy for users to understand. She also invested in advanced cybersecurity, including post-quantum encryption research, knowing that quantum computing could one day make current encryption obsolete.

Her foresight paid off sooner than expected. Two years later, a new regional law required financial apps to provide algorithmic transparency and give users the ability to opt out of automated decision-making. Because Leila's team had already built these capabilities, they were compliant from day one — while many competitors scrambled to update their systems.

Beyond regulations, Leila focused on **building trust as a brand value**. She launched a "Privacy Promise" campaign, explaining to users exactly how their data was handled and why certain information was collected. Customers responded positively, with many citing the company's openness as a reason they chose the app over others.

By anticipating the future of privacy rather than reacting to it, Leila positioned her company as a leader in responsible data practices. In an industry where trust was often lacking, she had turned privacy into a powerful competitive edge — and in doing so, ensured her business was ready for whatever came next in the evolving world of digital privacy.

Chapter 11: Building a Privacy-First Culture in Organizations

A privacy-first culture goes beyond regulatory compliance — it makes data protection a core organizational value. While laws like GDPR, CCPA, LGPD, and PIPEDA provide the minimum standards, businesses that treat privacy as part of their identity gain a significant competitive advantage. A privacy-first culture ensures that every employee, from executives to entry-level staff, understands the importance of protecting personal information and integrates that awareness into their daily work.

The foundation of a privacy-first culture begins with **leadership commitment**. Executives must lead by example, prioritizing privacy in decision-making and resource allocation. This includes funding privacy initiatives, supporting ongoing training, and ensuring that data protection officers or compliance teams have the authority to enforce policies. Without leadership buy-in, privacy programs often become superficial, existing only on paper.

Employee empowerment is the next critical component. All staff should understand the value of personal data, recognize potential privacy risks, and feel responsible for safeguarding it. This requires regular training tailored to each role. For example, marketing teams should understand consent rules, customer service teams should know how to respond to data requests, and IT teams should master secure data handling. Training should be practical, interactive, and updated regularly to reflect new laws and threats.

Privacy by design and default must be part of every project and product. This means considering privacy from the start — not as an afterthought — and setting systems to the most privacy-protective settings by default. For example, a new app feature should collect the minimum amount of data needed and have opt-in consent for additional processing. This principle ensures that privacy protections are built into the architecture of the business.

Creating a privacy-first culture also means fostering **transparency**. Customers should be clearly informed about what data is collected, why it is collected, and how it is used. Internally, employees should understand the company's data flows, security measures, and breach response procedures. Transparency builds trust and reduces the likelihood of misunderstandings that can lead to complaints or regulatory investigations.

Accountability mechanisms are essential. Regular privacy audits, clear reporting channels for suspected breaches, and documented data handling processes ensure that privacy is not left to chance. Recognizing and rewarding employees who identify privacy risks or suggest improvements reinforces positive behavior.

Finally, a privacy-first culture should embrace **continuous improvement**. Laws will evolve, new technologies will emerge, and customer expectations will shift. Businesses must remain adaptable, using feedback from employees, customers, and regulators to refine their privacy practices.

By embedding privacy into the DNA of the organization, companies not only comply with current laws but also future-proof themselves against emerging risks. More importantly, they signal to customers and partners that they can be trusted in an increasingly data-driven world.

Jasmine's story

Jasmine was the CEO of a fast-growing online education platform based in Melbourne. Her company served students in more than 30 countries, offering video courses, quizzes, and community forums. As the platform expanded, she noticed that questions about privacy began appearing in customer support tickets. Some students wanted to know how their progress data was stored, others asked whether their forum posts were visible to outsiders.

Initially, Jasmine thought these were isolated concerns. But after reading about a competitor's public relations crisis over a privacy breach, she realized that trust was becoming a major differentiator in the e-learning industry. She decided to make **privacy a core company value**, not just a legal requirement.

She started with her leadership team. In their next strategy meeting, Jasmine declared that privacy would be as important as product quality and customer service. She allocated a portion of the budget to hire a dedicated Data Protection Officer and authorized privacy training for every employee. This sent a clear message: privacy wasn't optional — it was part of their mission.

Next, she focused on **employee empowerment**. Rather than sending out a generic policy document, she organized interactive workshops. Developers learned how to code with privacy by design, limiting data collection and securing user uploads. Marketing staff practiced writing consent requests in plain, user-friendly language. Customer service agents role-played responding to data deletion requests under GDPR.

Jasmine also implemented **privacy by default** in product design. New features were reviewed by the DPO before launch, ensuring they collected only necessary data. For example, when adding a video transcription service, they decided not to store raw audio files longer than necessary, minimizing risk.

Transparency became a cornerstone of her brand. The privacy policy was rewritten in plain English, and the platform included a privacy dashboard where students could see what data was collected, download it, or request deletion with a single click. This not only met regulatory requirements but also boosted user confidence.

Over time, Jasmine saw a cultural shift. Employees began raising privacy considerations in meetings without being prompted. One developer suggested anonymizing certain analytics to reduce the risk of re-identification. Another proposed adding a privacy FAQ to the student onboarding process.

A year later, when the company applied for a large government contract to provide online training, their strong privacy culture became a deciding factor in winning the bid. The contract's evaluators noted that the company didn't just meet compliance standards — it exceeded them. Jasmine's commitment to building a privacy-first culture had transformed her business, strengthened customer trust, and positioned her platform as a leader in responsible online education.

Privacy as a Lifelong Commitment

In the fast-changing world of digital communication, privacy is no longer a luxury — it is a fundamental expectation. From the earliest days of the internet, when personal details were casually shared without much thought, to today's hyper-connected environment where every click, swipe, and search can be recorded, the importance of protecting personal information has grown exponentially. The lessons in this book are not meant to be a one-time checklist to "pass" compliance; they are the foundation for a lifelong commitment to respecting and safeguarding the privacy of those you serve.

The journey toward strong privacy practices begins with awareness. Understanding the global patchwork of laws — from GDPR in Europe to CCPA in California, LGPD in Brazil, PIPEDA in Canada, and emerging regulations across Africa, Asia, and the Middle East — is the first step. But compliance is not just about knowing the rules; it is about embedding them into the DNA of an organization. This requires a shift in mindset: from seeing privacy as a legal hurdle to embracing it as a competitive advantage and moral responsibility.

Technology will continue to evolve in ways that challenge existing frameworks. Artificial intelligence will become more predictive, blockchain will expand immutable recordkeeping, and quantum computing will test the limits of current encryption standards. Privacy laws will adapt, but innovation often moves faster than regulation. Organizations that anticipate these changes, prepare early, and remain adaptable will be the ones that thrive.

A privacy-first approach is also about human relationships. Every individual who provides their data — whether a customer, employee, student, patient, or citizen — is placing trust in the organization collecting it. Breaking that trust can have long-lasting consequences, both financially and reputationally. On the other hand, protecting that trust can lead to deeper loyalty, stronger partnerships, and sustainable growth.

The responsibility for privacy does not lie solely with governments or large corporations. Small businesses, startups, and individual professionals all play a role. In fact, smaller organizations often have the agility to implement strong privacy practices quickly, using them as a unique selling point against slower-moving competitors.

The most effective privacy strategies are built on three pillars: **transparency**, **security**, and **accountability**. Transparency means telling people what you are doing with their data in clear, honest terms. Security means implementing safeguards that are proportionate to the sensitivity of the information you handle. Accountability means being able to prove, at any moment, that you are living up to your commitments — not only because the law requires it, but because it is the right thing to do.

As you close this book, remember that privacy is not a static achievement but a living process. The laws will change. Technology will change. Your organization will change. But the principles outlined here — respecting personal data, limiting unnecessary collection, securing it from harm, and honoring the rights of individuals — are timeless. By making them a permanent part of your personal and professional ethos, you are not only protecting information; you are safeguarding the human dignity that lies at the heart of the digital age.

www.ingramcontent.com/pod-product-compliance
Ingram Content Group UK Ltd.
Pitfield, Milton Keynes, MK11 3LW, UK
UKHW020156290926
15471UKWH00005B/912